R47170
D1611076

Umrao Jaan

WADIA BROTH
Shree GANESH
श्री गणेश

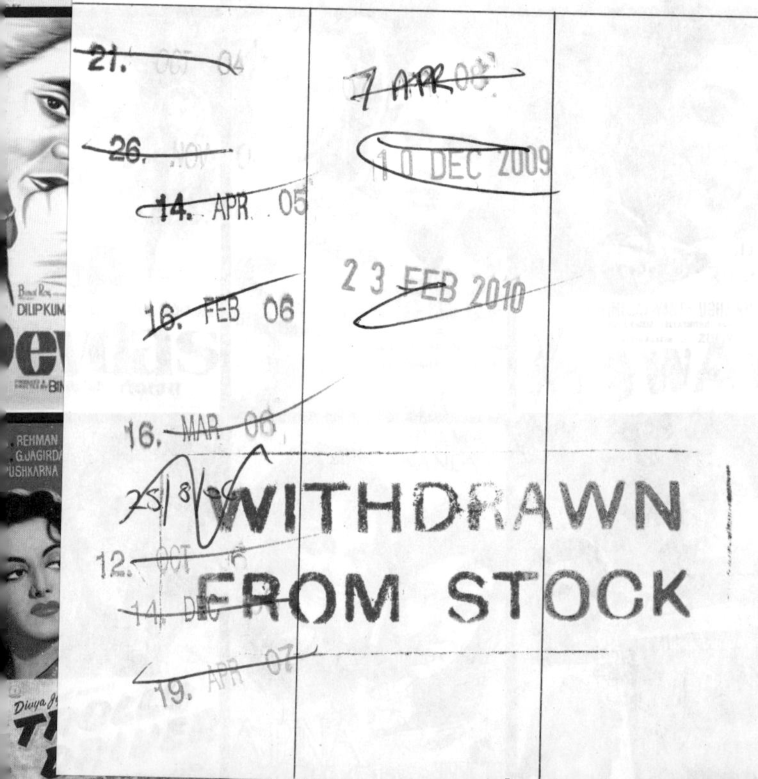

ANANDAN
RAMADOSS
CHELVARAJ
les mousquetaires indiens
(EL TALAT FORSANE)
LES TROIS BAGARREURS

# INDIAN BEAUTY

## BOLLYWOOD STYLE

601 West 26th Street, 18th floor
New York, NY 10001, USA
Tel.: 212 989-6810 Fax: 212 647-0005
www.assouline.com

First published by Editions Assouline, Paris, France.

Translated from the French by Deke Dusinberre.

Color separation: Gravor (Switzerland)
Printed by Grafiche Milani (Italy)

ISBN: 2 84323 572 3

BÉRÉNICE GEOFFROY-SCHNEITER

# INDIAN BEAUTY

## BOLLYWOOD STYLE

ASSOULINE

*For Edwige and Yvan Lagrange,*
*true lovers of Indian cinema*

*The important thing is not to see India the way it is, according to Europeans or Indians—which would be a silly goal, anyway. India must be viewed with the same preconceptions that French writers like Corneille and Barrès viewed Spain. It is by regarding India as an* imaginary land *that we come closest to reality. Nor would we want to regard it any other way.*
Jean Grenier (philosopher), *Les Îles*, 1933.

Mumbai (also known as Bombay): a sprawling metropolis, black with dust and grime, where motorbikes whine like insects and decrepit façades are plagued with electricity lines and TV antennas. And yet everywhere, you also see "them." They are bright and cheerful, dozens of feet high, with eyes alluringly outlined in kohl, and crimson lips that offer a bewitching smile. So who are "they"? They are the sweet, sexy posters that brashly sing the praises of the new movies just released by the city's film studios. Courtesans glittering with gold and gems, virtuous girls with tear-rimmed eyes, bandits and gangsters with sinister snarls, couples wrapped in an eternal embrace: nothing is too marvelous when it comes to making viewers forget their everyday cares and their grim lives. In India, more than anywhere else on the planet, the movies are still a religion, a true "opium of the people." This magic pill of intense emotions and guaranteed happiness is packed with obsessive melodies

and sultry dance routines. Produced by the thousands in Bombay's studios, these melodramatic epics have spawned a distinct style now identified by three sharp yet sugary syllables: "Bollywood." This skillful blend of kitsch and eroticism has not only conquered the theaters of India, but has also invaded screens in the Middle East, Europe, and Russia, and is even influencing art and fashion throughout the West!
What's the recipe? Take a classic old Indian movie, bring it up to date with a wedding-cake décor, add a riot of color and spice, then mix in some demonic bad guys (replete with mustaches) and a few bejeweled damsels in the form of a *maharani* or a spell-binding dancer whose swirling pirouettes are worthy of a stage-thumping musical.

It would be a serious mistake to underestimate the whirlwind created by movie-crazed India. Beneath the sea of patchouli and cardamom that so appeals to fans of exotic scents there lies an entire "archaeology of film." Movie-goers are offered a poetic, topsy-turvy patchwork of the most primal elements of theater and epic tale. In order to understand the true essence of this mystical, religious ritual, you have to attend an outdoor screening with all its noise and tumult. There, seated on bleachers (or sometimes right on the ground), men, women, and children boisterously commune with the object of their devotion—the god "Screen." All the ingredients of enthrallment are here: the wait, the wonder, the thrill, the fear. Today's film-makers, distant descendents of ancient poets and storytellers, have now attained the status of "celluloid bards."

Of course, the amorous adventures of Krishna, the blue-skinned god, still warm every Indian heart, and wonderful tales from the *Mahabharata* still inspire, indirectly, scores of films and productions. Nowadays, however, "idols" tend to take the form of beautiful actresses with flowing hair who display their erotic charms for fans who are overwhelmingly young and male. Greatly magnified by poster artists, their huge graven images proudly claim space alongside colorful depictions of the most popular Hindu gods.

Ravishing eyes, generous hips, supple waist, ample breasts: on close inspection, the anatomy of your average "screen goddess" turns out to incarnate the very essence of Indian aesthetics. Since the dawn of time, the Indian woman has been viewed as Mother Goddess, celestial nymph, nature deity. She embodies that vaguely dreaded cosmic power whose energy is the source of everything. "I am the Kingdom, the dispenser of riches, she who knows. I come first in all rites. Many are the homes the gods have given me. My empire is immense. I reside in all that is. From me comes forth all that is eaten, all that is seen, all that is breathed, all that is heard. Those who ignore me are destroyed. Listen then and meditate with respect on what I say. I am the joy of gods as well as of men. . . . My grandeur surpasses Heaven and Earth." (*Veda,* 8: 7, 125)

The voice that utters such haughty pronouncements comes from Shakti herself, the "power" or energy without which even the gods would be nothing but lifeless bodies lacking divinity. Many are her names, multiple her appearances. And yet she is "One," the source of everything. Veneration of Shakti dates back to primeval times when people worshiped crudely shaped clay idols that archaeologists quickly dubbed "fertility goddesses." Sometimes these figurines would feature outsized hips, buttocks, and breasts; other times they would take the form of a simple, polished stone daubed in red to evoke the menses of all-nourishing Mother Earth. Many centuries later there evolved the concept of *yakshi* (nature deities) and *apsaras* (celestial nymphs) whose voluptuous bodies, which grace the thresholds of temples and sanctuaries, symbolize both fertilizing energy and sacred eroticism.

True enough, perhaps no other civilization has so glorified the female principle as has India with its many religions. From frescoes in Ajanta to sensual statues on the temples of Khajuraho, woman is depicted as a heavenly incarnation who adopts the vigorous pose of an S-shaped curve, that is to say the energy-giving *tribhanga*. The curves and countercurves of these deities, as immortalized in stone, are described through metaphors borrowed from the animal and plant kingdoms: svelte body as supple as a vine, broad hips that sway like a chariot wheel, breasts firm and shapely like nectar-filled cups, arms as slender as lotus stems, legs tapered like those of a gazelle, thighs hale and hearty like the trunk of an elephant or banana tree. There is nothing profane, however, about these voluptuous bodies so overflowing with life—although they exude eroticism and fertility, *apsaras* and *yakshi* belong to another, non-human world. In their superterrestrial world, everything evokes Matisse's famous painting of *Luxe, calme, et volupté*: "Luxuriance, peace, pleasure." In their world, the sacred can be sexy; benevolent protection can be expressed by fleshly beauty. Every detail, from elaborate coiffure to abundant jewelry (simultaneously stressing the whiteness of the skin and curves of the body) contributes to make these "dream creatures" all the more desirable. Meanwhile, Bollywood—keen to sustain these visual and religious allusions—strives to perpetuate this ideal of woman who is both goddess and courtesan. It is even whispered here that under-endowed actresses go so far as to pad their bras in order to insure a mandatory resemblance to Hindu goddesses!

The fantasy of "generous, fertilizing beauty" perhaps found its most sophisticated expression in the sublime little paintings known as Mughal miniatures. Many artists deployed their lyrical brushwork to immortalize the "secret loves of victorious Krishna and Radha on the banks of the Yamuna River." Indeed, Hindu texts refer to Krishna, the young blue-skinned god, as the "Charming One," the "Moonlight of the World." A famous passage in the *Gita Govinda* proclaims: "His beauty was such that the sages themselves were aroused by it. Birds, wild cats, and other animals, insects, trees, and creeping vines trembled with desire to approach him, to touch him. Even the proud demons were charmed when they set eyes on him." Alas, many of the heroes of Bollywood's prolific output fail to live up to the airy grace of the young shepherd who could charm a whole swarm of pretty shepherdesses with the sound of his flute alone. The screens of Bombay, Trivandrum, and elsewhere are unfortunately overpopulated with pale copies afflicted with sagging flesh and drooping cheeks. Who cares! Bollywood celluloid manages to produce the same riot of color and zest that emanates from luminous Mughal miniatures. The same lovers make passionate confessions at nightfall, when the orb of the moon casts a gleaming halo around their pure vows. The same vines embrace trees, the same flowers unfold, and the same henna-dyed hands flutter and meet in the same not-very-veiled erotic allusions.

Although India gave birth to one of the most famous erotic poems in the world—the *Kama Sutra* with its countless positions and precepts—love on the screen remains strangely and totally chaste. There is no passionate groping, much less naked frolics. At most there will be a sensual "wet sari" number, wildly cheered by a young audience for the most part pure and innocent. The rather straightforward explanation is that a film can only be a popular hit if it pleases every member of the clan, from granny to grandson, from urban denizens to country folk. So boy meets girl, boys loses girl, and a hint of eroticism is heightened by a drop of moist sensuality—but that's it. Sometimes a close-up shot of slightly parted crimson lips will let informed viewers know that unbridled sex has just occurred. With their suggestive dances that avoid true contact, Bollywood movies are more about schmaltz than sex education. Ever since it was launched in Bombay in 1913, in fact, the "masala film" formula has religiously followed the same rules. Since it is designed to spellbind as well as to anaesthetize the masses, Bollywood cinema draws its love stories and demonic tales from Sanskrit theater and popular lore. The timeless recipe of success includes: six songs, at least three dance sequences, a running time of no less than three hours (usually capped by a happy ending), plus a good dose of a larger-than-life India that can be savored with the same pleasure thousands of miles away by families of the Indian diaspora scattered across London, New York, and Paris.

Much of Bollywood output, it must be admitted, has a hasty, do-it-yourself air, as reflected in videocassette wrappers with their syrupy colors and sloppy printing. These gaudy covers inevitably feature the face of a dark-eyed hero making a knowing wink as he clutches a patchouli clone of Sophia Loren or Ava Gardner. Yet herein lies the true nature of "cinemasala": a shameless mixture of kitsch and cheap eroticism, to be consumed as hastily as it was cooked up. Once again, we need to share the experience with an Indian family in order to appreciate the collective howls of laughter or anger triggered by often grotesque and sometimes lewd posturing. Everything is laid on thick for the audience—an ardent kiss against a setting sun, an exchange of oaths by the light of the moon, scenes of despair to music as drippy as the sets and costumes. In short, everything contributes to a tear-jerking extravaganza liable to move the hardest of hearts. Perhaps it all sums up India's fundamental ambivalence: a strange mixture of modesty and exhibitionism, of refinement and crudeness, of the sacred and the profane.
A different audience, meanwhile, enjoys "Bollywood magic" with the same enthusiasm and devotion—namely, movie-goers in the West who are only too happy to indulge in the facile exoticism and magical solutions of films that are simultaneously naïve and sophisticated. No festival worthy of the name now fails to include a "chic" Bollywood product. Taking the cue from Yimou Zhang's sprawling Shanghai films, flamboyant productions such as Mira Nair's *Kama Sutra, A Tale of Love* (1996) or, more recently,

Sanjay Leela Bhansali's *Devdas* (2002) have invaded Western screens and elevated the genre into the luxury-goods category. Here again, everything is done to string the new audiences along, playing on the languors of an India more imagined than real: magnificent sets straight out of the Thousand and One Nights, a carefully measured dose of exoticism and eroticism, and more complex, studied characters (played by celebrity-bound actors and especially actresses, notably exemplified by Aishwarya Rai, now ambassadress for the L'Oreal brand and a member of the jury at the latest Cannes Film Festival). Years ago Fritz Lang did exactly the same thing when he made his extravagant *Indian Tomb* (1959), set in a jungle of tigers and dancers. Renoir was a little more restrained with his *River* (1951), featuring a purely visual beauty and a timeless, languid pace. Meanwhile, with her ethereal *India Song* (1975), Marguerite Duras produced a typical example of, well—Duras, as usual.

India, nevertheless, was made in the image of its gods: ever-changing and ungraspable. It is like those episodic tales and movies with their age-old formulas. Behind the extravagant scowls and dripping make-up we can suddenly get a glimpse of the venerable, theatrical tradition of Kathakali dance; behind the gaudy colors and heavy fragrances we can recognize the shining nuptials of Radha and Krishna, the cosmic blaze of Vishnu or Shiva.

For fans of India, Bollywood carries the taste of Proust's famous madeleine—a sweetness that vacillates between delicious and sickly, between tantalizing and repellent.

# Bollywood from A to Z

## B

### Bombay

In Bombay (the colonial name for Mumbai), films are shot in Marathi—the local language—as well as in Gujarati and Punjabi. A majority of them are also made in Hindi, the most widely spoken language in the Indian Union. Labeled "All India," these movies literally flood the screens not only on the subcontinent but also in the Middle East and Russia. Westerners long considered these mass films as unworthy offshoots of Hollywood, which led to the more or less flattering label of "Bollywood." But many film buffs have begun to realize that certain films are noteworthy for their visual power, their deep roots in mythological and religious tradition, and above all the extreme virtuosity of their choreography and music. As an art that is both working-class and intellectual, the output from the Bombay studios includes not only commercial hits but real masterpieces such as *Mother India* (1957) and, more recently, the flamboyant *Lagaan: Once Upon a Time in India* (2001).

## D

### Dance

As anyone who has ever been to India knows, dance is viewed as sacred there—a dancer is a spiritual vehicle who offers a glimpse of the deity. Hence, there is nothing profane about dancing within the temple; each gesture is symbolic, each movement represents a dialogue between body and soul. Although every god in the

Hindu pantheon is occasionally depicted in a dancing pose (from Ganesh, the elephant-headed god, to Krishna, the charmer), it is Shiva who is considered the "Supreme Dancer." It is he who, through his cosmic dance, destroys and simultaneously re-creates the universe.
Heir to these ancient concepts, Bollywood films use—and abuse—dance sequences that can be extremely lascivious. Their erotic (indeed, orgasmic) aspect can hardly be overlooked. The screens of Bombay and elsewhere tolerate no trace of nudity or any passionate kissing, yet their languorous choreography is liable to make both male and female viewers swoon. By turns melancholic, sad, despairing, happy, and amorously ecstatic, these song-and-dance sequences function as a coded language that intensifies emotions and even substitutes for the sex act itself!

## Devdas

A famous novel by the great Bengali writer Saratchandra Chatterjee, *Devdas,* has already been brought to the silver screen more than fourteen times. The story is extremely straightforward: Devdas and Paro have loved one another since childhood, but cannot wed because they belong to different castes. The young woman is forced to marry a wealthy old man, so the male hero seeks to forget her in the arms of a beautiful courtesan, ultimately sinking into alcoholism and despair. *Devdas,* an authentic cry of outrage against the patriarchal social system, is striking in its fatal pessimism. The young man is portrayed as a puppet, the women as either inaccessible goddess or vamp (which has had a lasting influence on several generations of Indian filmmakers). The most recent version to date (2002), a magnificent fresco directed by Sanjay Leela Bhansali, brought to Western attention the sublime Aishwarya Rai, who has become a superstar.

# Directors

Some Bollywood directors have attained true fame, adored by film specialists and general public alike. In this context, Mehboob Khan, Guru Dutt, Bimal Roy, and Raj Kapoor might be considered the four musketeers of Hindustani cinema.

Khan, a great fan of Cecil B. DeMille, made dashing historical epics, including the legendary *Mother India* (1957), that country's *Gone with the Wind,* which even won Khan an Oscar nomination.

Actor, director, and producer Dutt, meanwhile, projected the image of a dark and tormented artist. The magic of his magnificent black-and-white films left a strong mark on the history of Indian cinema, creating the character of the romantic hero haunted by failure and death. Dutt himself committed suicide in 1964.

Originally from East Bengal (now Bengladesh), Roy got his start in Calcutta in the glamorous New Theatre studios. Heavily influenced by Italian neo-realist movies (such as Vittorio de Sica's *The Bicycle Thief* and the films of Rosselini), he made poignant films of great sobriety. His *Madhumati* (1955) was a disturbing tale of reincarnation, that religious belief at the very heart of Indian culture. As a great box-office hit, it reconciled commercial movies with art films.

Lastly, Kapoor, the famous heir to a filmmaking "dynasty," attacked every genre: glamour pics, mythological and historical epics (in 1940 he put in a remarkable performance as Alexander the Great in Sohrab Modi's *Sikander*), as well as melodrama and comedy. Having churned out over seventy films, he is above all loved by Indians as a kind of avatar of Charlie Chaplin, whom he could mimic down to the tiniest gestures and expressions.

More recently, the young filmmaker Mira Nair (born in 1957 of

Punjabi parents) is perhaps the most famous female Indian director abroad. Having abandoned the documentary style of her first film, *Salaam Bombay!* (winner of the Gold Camera Award at Cannes in 1988), she has since made two films much closer to the Bollywood aesthetic: the chic and icy *Kama Sutra, A Tale of Love* (1997) and the more sensual and lively *Monsoon Wedding* (Golden Lion at Venice in 2001). Her critics complain that Nair now makes movies for Westerners in search of "exotic chic and shock."

# F

## Family

The family plays a central role in India, both in real life and in the movies. There have been an infinite number of patchouli Romeos and Juliettes, countless bloody, fratricidal struggles worthy of the house of Atreus. Playing on the phenomenon of viewer identification, Bollywood films usually act as a balm on the internal tensions of a society torn between modernity and respect for tradition.

# G

## Gangsters

Steeped in American and Asian influences, Bollywood productions teem with outlaws and crooks who range from petty hoodlums in the poorest parts of town to organized criminals of the highest order. These violent, crowd-pulling box-office hits are nevertheless threatened by foreign competition. In a more specifically "Indian" vein, Shekhar Kapur's *Bandit Queen* (1994) immortalized the figure of a lower-caste gang leader who terrorized central India in a bold embodiment of the revolt of rural outlaws against poverty and government authorities.

## Hollywood

Even when seasoned with masala sauce, Hollywood is still the ultimate model for Bollywood, which serves up the same musicals, the same love-struck heroes, the same capricious stars, the same wonderful sets, and above all the same magical formulas for grown-up children (whether "ketchup" or "curry" flavor).

I

## Indomania

Artists and intellectuals have always been fascinated by India, as witnessed by retrospectives of Satyajit Ray's films at the Cinémathèque Française, by Peter Brook's stage production of the *Mahabharata,* and even by Marguerite Duras's ghostly film *India Song*. Distinct from this respectful veneration is an "Indomania" that has wildly gripped fashion and design in recent years, filtering down to people in the street. Posters, album covers, home-decoration mags, and even haute couture fashion shows (as exemplified by John Galliano's recent collection) have reinvented a colorful, festive India wreathed in scents of incense and patchouli. However, this bazaar aesthetic is based more on collective fantasy than on reality (as colorful as that reality may be).

## Kitsch

Diehard purists often criticize Bollywood for its sickly sweet formulas and its "supermarket" fetishism. That attitude reflects a basic misconception of what gives a Bollywood movie its true flavor—the image of a larger-than-life India that has inherited the most noble features of kitsch: brash colors, extravagant sets, and glittery gold and jewels straight out of *A Thousand and One Nights*, yielding a hybrid offspring of Broadway musicals and Mughal miniatures.

# L

## Love

The heart often throbs in your average Bollywood film, triggered by unrequited love, by family feuds worthy of the bitterest Greek tragedies, by secret love affairs between members of different castes, or by a lover lost, regained, betrayed. Against a background of tear-jerking melodrama, the silver screen thus presents a true reflection of Indian society trapped in archaic conventions and contradictions. Here people learn that marriage is rarely "for love," but is rather a question of convenience, not to say resignation.

## Mumbai

See B for Bombay.

## Mythology

The aesthetics and narrative structure of Bollywood films are based on the ancient, mythical texts of the *Mahabharata* and the *Ramayana,* those colorful, epic tales. Following the tradition of poets and story-tellers who recited such tales in villages and palaces, filmmakers devised spectacles capable of expressing all the power of dreams and marvelous events. In short, they developed a total art form in which music, song, and dance combine to intoxicate the senses—and sometimes even make viewers stop and think. Indeed, Bollywood cinema could be seen as a modern, psychoanalytic version of the most ancient of myths.

# S

## Schmaltz

With their clear-cut good guys and bad buys, simplistic plots, and happy endings, Bollywood movies often come across as fairy tales for adults. The outcome is thoroughly predictable: boy gets girl back, parents are proud and happy, the bad guys get caught and put in jail. As a buffer between desire and reality, these films often serve as a pain-killer for an entire society, as mass-consumed candy both sweet and sickening. Yet as a source of fantasies, they wonderfully awaken the child in us all.

## Song

In India, people say the movies are just an excuse to make music. True enough, their country boasts one of the richest musical traditions in the world, dating back over five thousand years. Almost every private event or celebration, such as a birth or wedding, is accompanied by its own special type of music. A movie's weak storyline is thus often bolstered by a wave of songs that pace the action—indeed, prolong it. Western viewers accustomed to a linear narrative are sometimes surprised by the sudden interruption of a song with no direct link to the dramatic action. Yet the role of song is very specific, namely to create a certain emotional state. It is also an indirect way of including a measure of eroticism in a country where censorship forbids any "realistic" contact between bodies.

Another significant detail involves recordings: tens of millions of cassettes of these songs circulate well before a film is released—and long after—representing a vast source of profit for producers and performers.

## Star System

India is probably the last country in the world where actors have retained their mythical aura, just like the superstars during Hollywood's golden age. Even at a time when television and video are threatening the god "Movie," new stars are being born every day. Some Indian actresses have attained the same heights as Marilyn Monroe and Greta Garbo did in their day, including Waheeda Rehman (who stars in Guru Dutt's films) and Nargis (the soul of Raj Kapoor's movies). Nor are men excluded from the phenomenon of collective hysteria, which sometimes recalls the magic of primitive worship and ancestral rites. The mere presence of Hindi superstar Amitabh Bachchan can provoke a riot of tens of thousands of fans. Dev Anand, meanwhile, was nicknamed "the Indian Cary Grant." The most recent starburst comes from the sublime Aishwarya Raj, who conquered hearts in Bombay before ravaging London, New York, and Paris. "She's worth it," claims the slogan of the cosmetic company she now represents.

## Studio System

The Indian film industry boasts a prodigious output—seven to eight hundred movies per year, far more than are made in Europe or the United States. Indian studios first appeared in the 1920s, springing up in major port towns such as Bombay, Calcutta, and Madras. One of the most famous firms was the Kohinoor Film Company, founded in 1918 by Dwarkadas N. Sampat, who dared, in his very first year, to show a woman in a state of undress! Based on permanent crews who were paid monthly and who could perform every task, Indian studios were soon creating the first silent screen stars whose status rivaled that of their Hollywood counterparts. While the big companies in Bombay shot films in Marathi, Gujarati, and Punjabi, Calcutta aimed its films primarily at north-western regions (Bengal, Assam, Orissa), and Madras was the main filmmaking hub for the southern states of Tamil Nadu, Kerala, and Karnataka. Soon, however, movies shot in Hindi (the most widespread language) and labeled "All India Films" could be seen on screens everywhere, even monopolizing the export market. And so the "Bollywood" phenomenon was born.

## Woman

To the great misfortune of women in India, Bollywood movies often simply perpetuate the phallocratic vision of Indian society. On screen as in life, a woman must be either daughter, wife, mother, or courtesan. Worse, "modern" women are often portrayed as being a threat to the social order. Bombay productions know no shades of gray: it's either wholesome mother/goddess or venomous femme fatale. A new trend is beginning to emerge, however, granting star actresses stronger roles with more psychological complexity. From Mahesh Bhatt's *Arth* (1983), which recounted the rebellion of an abandoned wife, to Mira Nair's *Monsoon Wedding* (2001), women are finally beginning to take their fates into their own hands.

HOMI WADIA *Presents* WADIA BROTHE
PRODUCTION

# Shree GANESH

# श्री गणेश

music: BULO C. RANI ✶ Directed by: S.S.DHARWADKA

1931.

BHANSALI
a SANJ

# Chronology

**1896:** The first projection of moving pictures in India was held on July 7, at the Watson Hotel in Bombay. The Lumière brothers' new invention was hailed by the *Times of India* as "the wonder of the century."

**1913:** The first Indian fiction film, *Raja Harishchandra,* by D.G. Phalke, was based on a mythological subject. The golden age of silent cinema had begun. Unfortunately, many of the films shot in those days have vanished (over 1,200).

**1929:** The Prabhat Film Company, which produced films in the Marathi language, was founded near Bombay.

**1930:** New Theatres, Ltd., was founded in Calcutta. The company would release the first screen adaptation of *Devdas,* directed by P.C. Barua.

**1931:** The talkies arrived in India with *The Light of the World,* shot in Hindi by Ardeshir Irani. It was a period of extravagant musicals inspired by Sanskrit theater and India's founding myths. At the same time, political issues came to the fore alongside India's emerging nationalist movement.

**1934:** The great producer Himansu Rai founded Bombay Talkies.

**1940-1950:** The majors lost ground to independent producers. Studios began to imitate the Hollywood model, paying vast salaries to famous stars.

**1947-1960:** Political consciousness continued to rise during India's transition to independence. The desire to build a new nation was reflected in Mehboob Khan's *Mother India* (1957).

**1960-1970:** Indian producers began to seek foreign markets. Fashionable themes included the "young generation" and its desire for sexual liberation—posters even made daring psychedelic allusions!

**1970-1980:** In the context of political strife and a rise in urban violence, Indian movies began to portray male heroes who had to grapple with their own fate. One of Bollywood's most popular stars emerged—Amitabh Bachchan.

**1980-2004:** An upscale Bollywood style was cultivated, aimed at Western audiences. This trend is exemplified by Mira Nair's recent films, *Kama Sutra, a Tale of Love* (1997) and *Monsoon Wedding* (2001), as well as by the latest, lavish version of *Devdas* (2002), directed by Sanjay Leela Bhansali.

*Satyajit Ray's legendary film* The Music Room *(1958) perhaps represents the antithesis of the Bollywood aesthetic.*
*© Satyajit Ray Films/Kobal Collection.*

*From the back of the room, where she was somewhat hidden in the shadows, she came forward, a creature all in gold and jewels, setting off sparks; she came upon me, indignant and accusing, eyes full of anger and menace; she blocked me, intimidating me with sweeping gestures that called upon the gods as her witness to some crime I had allegedly committed. Then, all of a sudden, this dancing-girl burst into laughter, supremely mocking, pouring disdain all over me, pointing me out to the mirthful crowd. Her irony was every bit as contrived as her haughty imprecations had been, just seconds before. How marvelous was her mimicry. Bitter laughter rang from deep in her throat, somewhat dark in timbre. And she laughed with her mouth, with her eyes, her brows, her chest, her leaping breasts. As she moved off, in hysterics, it was overpowering—you just had to laugh, too.*

Pierre Loti, *L'Inde (sans les Anglais)*, 1903

# Select Bibliography


*Indomania: le cinéma indien des origines à nos jours.* Paris: Cinémathèque Française/Musée du Cinéma, 1995.

Kabir, Nasreen Munni, and Jonathan Torgovnik (photographer). *Bollywood Dreams: An Exploration of the Motion Picture Industry and Its Culture in India.* London: Phaidon, 2003.

Kabir, Nasreen Munni (ed). *Les Stars du cinéma indien.* Paris: Centre Georges Pompidou/Centre national de la Cinématographie, 1985.

Mishra, Vijay. *Bollywood Cinema, Temples of Desire.* New York/London: Routledge, 2001.

Passek, Jean-Loup (ed). *Le Cinéma Indien.* Paris: Centre Georges Pompidou/L'Equerre, 1983.

Thoraval, Yves. *Les Cinéma de l'Inde.* Paris: L'Harmattan, 1998.

Vasudev, Aruna and Philippe Lenglet (eds). *Les Cinémas indiens.* Paris: CinémAction/Éditions du Cerf, 1984.


# Select Web Sites

www.b4utv.com
www.beena.com
www.bollywood.de
www.bollywood-boulevard.com
www.bollywoodworld.com
www.ebolly.com
www.stardustindia.com

Devdas *by Sanjay Bhansali, 2002. Here we see Paro, the heroine, portrayed by Bollywood star Aishwarya Rai.*
*© Les Archives du 7ᵉ art.*

# Indian Beauty Bollywood Style

**Smita Patil in** ***Manthan*** *(The Churning)* by Shyam Benegal (1975). © All rights reserved.
**Female deity,** early 9th century, sandstone. Khajuraho style, northern India. Musée des Arts Asiatiques–Guimet, Paris. © H. Lewandowski/RMN.
Bollywood movies use—and abuse—archetypes of Indian beauty as found in the large stone statues on the temples at Khajuraho: generous hips, ample breasts, and a supple waist that weaves like a snake or a vine.

**Nalini Jaywant,** a star of the 1950s. © All rights reserved.
***Kama Sutra, A Tale of Love*** by Mira Nair (1997). © Les Archives du 7e art.
Half a century separates these two Indian films, yet they share the same inspiration and aesthetics, as do the two actresses in the guise of maharanis.

**Young Indian woman** in ceremonial dress. Mumbai, India, 1993. © Steve McCurry/Magnum.
**Young Indian woman,** 18th-century miniature, Jaipur school. Sangaram Singh Collection, Jaipur. © Jean-Louis Nou/AKG Paris.
In this glittering photo of a bride, American photographer Steve McCurry has reincarnated the sophisticated palette of the finest Mughal miniatures.

**Earrings and nose ornament,** 19th century, gold, pearls, diamonds, emeralds, rubies. Northern India. Musée des Arts Asiatiques–Guimet, Paris. © T. Ollivier/RMN.
***Kama Sutra, A Tale of Love*** by Mira Nair (1997). © Les Archives du 7e art.
Serious film buffs accuse director Mira Nair of producing Bollywood movies aimed solely at Western audiences, thanks to slick imagery, "exportable" actors, and a dose of "exotic chic and shock"—in short, a calculated recipe for success.

**Braided hair and flowers,** January 1993. Chidambaram, Tamil Nadu. Indian women, especially in the south, almost always adorn their hair with flowers. © Roland et Sabrina Michaud/Rapho.
***Monsoon Wedding*** by Mira Nair, 2001. © Mirabai Films/Delhidotcom/Kobal Collection.
Mira Nair's *Monsoon Wedding* won the Golden Lion at Venice in 2001 and is a paean to the magnificence of India. Bedecked with flowers and jewelry, the heroine looks like a photonovel princess (though with an added pinch of humor).

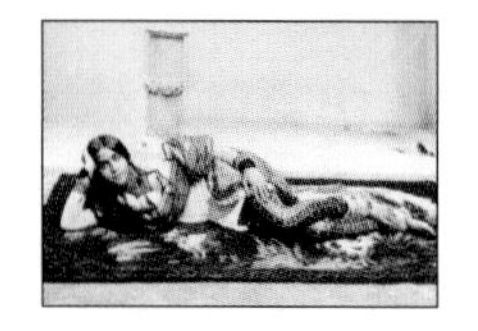

**An Indian odalisque,** 19th century. © Rue des Archives.
With her "serpentine" elegance, this young woman closely resembles the "dream creatures" described by travel writer Pierre Loti when he reached India in the early twentieth century.

**Four women,** 18th century, paint on canvas. Kishangarh, India. Musée des Arts Asiatiques–Guimet, Paris. © Arnaudet/RMN.
***Kama Sutra, A Tale of Love*** by Mira Nair (1997). © Rue des Archives.
One of Bollywood's favorite clichés is a scene in which the female star is caught bathing. The same charming scene of undress can be found in many lively little miniatures.

***Shree Ganesh,*** poster, circa 1960. © Swim Ink/Corbis.
**Prithviraj Kapoor in *Mughal-E-Azam*** (*Emperor of the Mughals*) by K. Asif (1960). © All rights reserved.
Divine fury and terror: whether conveyed through gaudy posters in the streets of Mumbai or through the bloodshot eyes of Bollywood actors, magnificent violence is ever-present. India may be the land of Gandhi, but it also worships the god known as Shiva the Destroyer.

**Princess doing her hair,** 18th century, gouache with gold highlights on paper. India. Musée du Louvre, Paris. © H. Lewandowski/RMN.
**Girls bathing.** Tamil Nadu, southern India. © Jean-Louis Nou/AKG Paris.
An Indian version of the concept of "Eternal Womanhead" as recorded by the delicate brush of a painter of miniatures and by the admiring camera of a great photographer, Jean-Louis Nou. Here, unconstrained hair symbolizes the height of abandon.

***Kama Sutra, A Tale of Love*** by Mira Nair (1997). © Rue des Archives.
Another typical Bollywood ploy is an erotic scene that ultimately remains oh-so-chaste! In India, there's no getting around the censor.

**A Muslim woman** smoking a hookah. © Rue des Archives.
***The Chess Players*** by Satyajit Ray (1977). © Les Archives du 7ᵉ art.
These two creatures, puffing dreamily on their hookahs, may look to us like hookers, but we should remember that northern India was never far from the land of *A Thousand and One Nights*.

**"Answering with a smile."** Rama's wife Sita simply smiled, rather than uttering a word. Gouache on paper, third quarter of the 17th century, Basohli workshop, Pahari school. Dogra Art Gallery, Jammu. **Dancing girl.** Indian miniature, Jaipur. Sangaram Singh Collection. **"Awaiting the tryst."** A *nayika* ("heroine in love") awaits her lover on a terrace. Gouache on paper, second quarter of 17th century, Bagda-Chokha family workshop, Deogarh, Rajasthan. Patna Museum. © Jean-Louis Nou/AKG Paris. Dance as both sacred art and sensual delight: three bayaderes, or dancing women, with exquisite bodies that move to the same tune.

**On a set in Bombay** (Mumbai), 1993. © Steve McCurry/Magnum.
Feverish preparations on a set in a Bombay studio. It's all here—the excitement, chaos, the star surrounded by make-up artists and assistants. Any minute now, the director will shout, "Action!"

**Shooting a film** in the R.K. studios, 1961. © Time Life Pictures/Getty Images.
***Kali Yug, Goddess of Vengeance*** by Mario Camerini (1963). © Les Archives du 7e art.
Bollywood's schmaltzy musicals often seem wonderfully kitsch, as exemplified by this parody of a sacred dancer portrayed by French actress Claudine Auger!

**Indian musicians and dancers** in traditional dress. Photograph by Horst P. Horst, circa 1950. © Condé Nast Archive/Corbis.
**A bayadere, or dancing girl.** Indian miniature, watercolor, 1831. Bibliothèque Nationale, Paris. © Visioars/AKG Paris.
India is the land of dance par excellence, because dance is said to regenerate the universe by unleashing cosmic, fertilizing forces. It is no coincidence that Shiva is still worshipped in the form of Nataraja, "Lord of the Dance."

***Gopi Vastraharan*** (stealing the cowherds' clothing). © All rights reserved.
***Kama Sutra, A Tale of Love*** by Mira Nair (1997). © Rasa Film/NDF International/Kobal Collection.
All children in India know the wonderful tale of Krishna, the young, blue-skinned shepherd-god who mischievously steals the clothes of the female cowherds in order to enjoy their splendid nakedness. Movie-goers indulge in similar "voyeurism" when admiring these divine creatures on the silver screen.

**Waheeda Rehman** in *Pyaasa (Thirst)* by Guru Dutt (1957). © All rights reserved.
***Sita Haran*** (the abduction of Sita). © All rights reserved.
The sublime Waheeda Rehman was cast as a mysterious, sacred figure in the films of her pygmalion of a director, Guru Dutt. A similar theatricality can sometimes be detected in the cheap color prints so prized by Indians.

**Poster workshop in Bombay** (Mumbai), 1993. © Steve McCurry/Magnum.
Bollywood posters constitute an industry that has forged its own artistic idiom based on bold colors and a refined sense of kitsch and impact. They are increasingly sought after by Western collectors and were even the object of a fascinating exhibition at London's Victoria and Albert Museum in 2002.

**Woman awaiting her lover.** Indian miniature, Rajput-Bikaner school, Rajasthan. Musée des Arts Asiatiques–Guimet, Paris. © Arnaudet/RMN.
***Kama Sutra, A Tale of Love*** by Mira Nair (1997). © Les Archives du 7e art.
Love, more love, and yet more love! The formula has hardly changed down through the ages—nor has the visual style!

**Tree-deity.** 10th/11th-century sculpture in the round, sandstone. Madhya Pradesh or Rajasthan. Musée des Arts Asiatiques–Guimet, Paris. © H. Lewandowski/RMN.
***Chandralekha*** by S. S. Vasan (1948). © All rights reserved.
Whether courtesan or *apsara* (celestial nymph), women are usually portrayed in Bollywood films as inaccessible creatures somewhere between vamps and demons. Recently, however, a few courageous directors have begun challenging this cliché.

**Henna-decorated hands** of a bride. Jaipur, Rajasthan. © Getty Images.
**The Goddess Durga,** 1931. Lithograph. © Bettmann/Corbis.
Beauty is somehow "larger than life" in India, whether measured by the intensity of color and scent or by the number of heads and arms, as seen in dazzling ceremonial make-up and an inexpensive color print.

***Tiger of Bengal*** by Fritz Lang (1958). © Les Archives du 7ᵉ art.
There is a long list of Western directors who became fascinated with India's exotic and poisonous charm. Fritz Lang was one who fell for this "mirage" that nevertheless yielded two of his most aesthetically accomplished movies.

***Bombay Dreams.*** West End musical, London, 2003. © Bombay Dreams TM/2002 RUG Ltd/Photograph by James Bareham.
A trip to London's West End theater district to enjoy a performance of *Bombay Dreams,* the first Bollywood-style stage musical, provides a good idea of the sociological and aesthetic scope of the new phenomenon as measured by the audience: the screams of teenage girls—usually dressed in saris—and the full-throated laughter of adults are visually accompanied by a riot of gold and jewelry. A Bollywood movie "for real"!

**A poster for *Devdas,*** photographed in Mumbai, 2002. © Noshir Desai/Corbis.
Rising above everyday grime is the splendid face of the latest Bollywood superstar, Aishwarya Rai, a former Miss World. Directed by Sanjay Bhansali, the latest film version of *Devdas* cost nearly twelve million dollars—an extravagance that matches the aspirations of worshipers of the god "Cinema."

**Krishna and Radha,** illustration from Song XII of the *Gita Govinda* by Bengali court poet Jayadeva, 12th century. Gouache on paper, Pahari school, 1730. Chandigarh Museum. © Jean-Louis Nou/AKG Paris. ***Devdas*** by Sanjay Bhansali, with Aishwarya Rai. © Les Archives du 7ᵉ art. It would be an understatement to say that India has produced some of the most famous and scandalous erotic poetry. And yet Bollywood films are surprisingly chaste, indeed puritanical. That is because they are aimed at mass audiences from all walks of life, from the youngest viewer to the oldest, the most innocent to the most experienced…

The author would particularly like to thank Martine Assouline for backing this project, Julie David for bringing it to life, Véronique, Jean-François, Mathilde, Anatole and François Hutin for their Bollywood hospitality, and Laurent and Cassandre Schneiter for their loving support.
The publisher would like to thank Fabienne Grévy (AKG Photo), Xavier B. Boquet (Archives du 7e art), Marie Campagne (British Tourist Office), Paul Tucker (The Really Useful Group), and the photographic agencies Corbis, Getty, Kobal, Magnum, Rapho, Rue des Archives.